# THE GOOGLE ADS BIBLE

# FOR BEGINNERS 2024

Gain Mastery in Driving Sales, Leads
Conversion, Brand Visibility, Stay on
Budget, Optimize ROI, and Reach Your
Customers Easily

*Sarah Jordan*

# COPYRIGHT PAGE

The author and publisher of this book are not responsible for how the information contained within it is used or abused. It is advised that readers communicate with certified experts or consultants in the field of advertising or marketing to solve specific issues or requirements.

# Table of Contents

Google Ads is the lifeblood of contemporary advertising in the huge digital void, throbbing with possibilities and difficulties. From its simple AdWords beginnings to the sophisticated, AI-infused marketing behemoth it is today is a tale of invention and adaptability.

It's like trying to make sense of a complicated tapestry that's weaved together out of marketing theory, consumer psychology, and cutting-edge technology.

Think of this hub as an active marketplace, a bazaar of keywords where companies compete to get their message heard above the din of online discourse. But it's more than simply a numbers game; it's also about picking up on the subtleties, the pulse of customer intent, and synchronizing them with the core of their products.

Here in this busy marketplace, keywords are the means of exchange. It's not enough to just recognize these linguistic nuggets; rather, the skill is in anticipating the user's next move by reading the unspoken signals of meaning in their queries.

Putting these terms together in ad groups is like composing music; it's all about striking the right balance between the user's needs and the advertiser's offering.

In today's bustling digital market, ad copy are the equivalent of bright banners blowing in the breeze. You need more than just a way with words to create effective banners; you need to construct an image that not only stands out, but also fits naturally into the story of the user's journey.

Advertisers can aim their messages like trained archers striking bullseyes in a whirling, ever-changing wind thanks to targeting, the marketplace's directional compass.

This sort of targeting goes much beyond simple demographics into a deeper familiarity with the requirements and wants of individual users.

This marketplace's bidding methods are a lot like the art of bargaining. Advertisers in this world don't only use cryptocurrency; they also use data and algorithms informed by machine learning to outbid one another for prime real estate.

However, this market is more than simply a location to buy necessities; it also serves as a magnificent venue for innovative shows.

Fireworks like ad extensions, adaptable search advertisements, and dynamic features aren't just meant to grab people's attention; they're meant to captivate and keep it.

However, the dance of data and insights is what really matters in this massive economy. In order to truly connect with their target audience, advertisers need to become interpreters of the crowd's reactions to their ads through the use of analytics and conversion monitoring.

Challenges arise in this convoluted economy. The threat of competition lingers over the smaller merchants like the shadows of tall buildings. Cost increases act like gusts of wind that threaten to tilt the banners, necessitating regular adjustments and optimization to remain upright.

However, tremendous opportunities lay inside these difficulties. The worldwide reach of Google Ads provides companies of all sizes with a level playing field on which to attract customers from all around the world.

Because it is possible to create stories of such grandeur that they move people to action and change their hearts and minds.

In today's competitive market, where innovation and creativity are intertwined, it's not enough to know how to use the tools; you also need to know how to conduct the symphony, coordinating the many parts into a whole that will leave your audience spellbound.

To master Google Ads, it's not enough to be good with numbers and code; you need to put on your artist's cap, step onto the digital stage, and use your strategic and creative chops to paint stories that strike a chord with your audience and motivate them to take action.

## How Google Ads Evolved

Google Ads' development throughout time exemplifies how far advertising technology has come and how quickly it can adapt to a changing digital world. The original Google AdWords was a simple advertising platform, but it has now evolved into a complex, AI-driven behemoth that has revolutionized the way brands interact with their customers.

This developing story has its roots in the early 2000s, when the internet was still mostly unexplored and search engines were emerging as entry points to this new world.

Google, with its purpose to collect the world's knowledge and make it widely accessible and useful, delved into the embryonic field of internet advertising with AdWords.

The initial idea was brilliantly straightforward: create a system where companies could compete for advertising space next to search results by bidding on certain keywords. This innovative idea was just the beginning of what would grow into a massive platform that would revolutionize the advertising industry.

Google's perspective grew along with the scope of the internet. Once limited to text advertising in SERPs, the platform has expanded to include a wide variety of ad formats throughout Google's network of sites and those of its partners.

With this growth came new types of advertisements, such as display ads, YouTube video campaigns, app ads, and even experimental shopper ad forms. Google Ads evolved from a practical resource for businesses to a limitless medium for expression and narrative.

It would be impossible to overestimate the significance of this change. It's not only about the shift in features and functions, but a paradigm shift in how businesses and consumers participate in the digital marketplace.

Google Ads evolved as a solution for companies to transcend the geographical barriers that were previously present in advertising. It leveled the advertising playing field, so that small businesses could compete with big conglomerates for the same audience.

It completely altered the customer experience of seeking out new goods and services. Users were presented with advertisements as well as personalized options that catered to their specific wants and requirements.

The incorporation of AI and ML into Google Ads is arguably the most ground-breaking development in this narrative of progress. These innovations were a watershed moment, ushering in a new age in which predictive analytics, clever bidding techniques, and individualized ad experiences could flourish on the platform.

The incorporation of AI didn't just automate processes; it enhanced them, making campaigns more efficient, targeting more accurate, and ad experiences more relevant.

As a result, marketers can now use data to inform their decisions and create campaigns that truly connect with their target demographic.

Connecting companies with their target audiences is where Google Ads really shines. It's not just about commercials; it's about narrative, about making links where there seem to be none. It's a platform for companies to do more than simply sell; they can also inform and enthrall customers.

This development is an exciting adventure; the meeting point of cutting-edge technology, savvy marketing, and an in-depth comprehension of consumer psychology. This story can teach us a lot about staying current in the digital age via flexibility, creativity, and perseverance.

The history of Google Ads is more than just a tale of technological advancement; it's a saga that redraws the boundaries of advertising, ushering in an era in which brands no longer merely sell products but also curate experiences, cultivating relationships, and weaving tales that strike a chord with consumers.

## How to Set Up A Google Ads Account

Setting up a Google Ads account is like the first crescendo in a symphony; it's the vital overture that paves the way for future advertising efforts to succeed. Setting the foundation for a smooth and productive voyage through the world of internet advertising is analogous to priming a canvas before painting a masterpiece.

Establishing a web presence, or "digital storefront," to promote your business to the large internet population is where your Google Ads campaign should begin.

The central step is creating an account, a virtual container for all of your professional goals and aspirations. It's a virtual nexus that enables you to use the powers of Google's advertising platform in your quest to reach and interact with your target audience.

Creating an account and setting it up is the first step in the setup procedure. Setting the scene entails establishing the parameters of your organization, deciding which regions to focus on, and settling on a currency and time zone.

The next step is to familiarize oneself with Google Ads' complex user interface. Exploring the many realms and options available is like setting out on a voyage through a detailed map. Learning the intricacies of the dashboard, from planning a campaign to seeing data, is like learning a new language.

This online fortress is built on a foundation of keywords and strategic campaign design. Finding the right keywords to describe your brand, learning how customers use your products, and organizing your campaigns so that you can effectively manage and target those keywords are all part of this process. It's like planting a seed for your brand in the digital landscape and tending to it so that it may develop and flourish.

This setting, however, isn't just about preparing the ground; rather, it's about building the foundation for a fruitful effort. Setting up your ad groups, ads, and landing pages is similar to painting a room; you want to use bold colors that represent your brand's personality and interest your target audience.

The financial components, including the cost of your advertising canvas and selecting the best methods to use your resources for greatest impact, may be arranged by configuring options like budget allocation and bidding tactics.

However, the most important factor in this complex preparation is vision; that is, knowing what you want to do and who you want to reach. It's not only about telling a story about your company; it's also about telling a tale about your clients and how your firm can help them achieve their goals.

Setting up a Google Ads account is not simply a mechanical procedure but an artful curation—a purposeful blend of technology and creativity. It's about building a digital identity for your company that beats to the same drum as your customers' hopes and dreams.

of this great spectacle, creating a Google Ads account is more than just a formality; it's the first act of a story arc that will weave together your brand's history and the experiences of the people you're trying to reach.

## How to Create and Configure Your Account

Setting up a Google Ads account is like laying the foundation for a physical building; it's the first step in your online advertising journey and signals the beginning of your online presence.

The first step is to establish your company's digital identity, or "digital footprint," in the enormous digital universe. To an ever-changing internet audience, it is akin to building the outside appearance of a colossal structure that embodies your brand's beliefs and objectives.

The process of setting up requires careful attention to minute details, like a ballet in which every move and nuance of information counts. The first steps are to register your company's information, decide where you want to focus your marketing efforts, and choose the local currency and time zone. These early setups are analogous to laying the groundwork, determining the bounds within which your digital kingdom will operate.

Learning your way around the Google Ads interface is like being shown the keys to your digital castle. You'll find everything you need to dominate the online marketplace here, from tools and settings to tips and tricks. Understanding the dashboard, from campaign design to viewing performance metrics, is like understanding the language of this new digital frontier.

Choosing the proper keywords is like painting a picture using your brand's palette; each color represents a term that will appeal to a specific demographic. The journey that potential buyers take to learn about and interact with your business is mapped out by these keywords.

Creating a plan for your account's campaigns and ad groups is similar to designing a blueprint for your virtual home. The goal is to set up a system that allows your advertising to expand and develop over time. Ad groups are like distinct wings of your digital palace; they each include advertisements that are relevant to a certain set of keywords.

Allocating your advertising budget, creating your bidding strategy, and setting limitations to guarantee best utilization of resources are all aspects of configuration. It's about making sure that every dollar you spend is a note in your advertising symphony.

But at the center of all those settings is your account's beating heart: the vision and plan that directs your work. Having a clear vision of your end result, your USP, and the experiences you wish to create for your target audience is essential.

When you create and configure your Google Ads account, you're not simply creating an account; you're building a digital home for your business. It's a finely woven tapestry of information and hopes, designed to speak to the hopes and dreams of your target audience.

In this complex tango of making and setting, you're not just creating an account; you're creating a digital narrative—a virtual storybook that caters to the desires and interests of your target demographic and compels them to investigate, interact with, and ultimately become an integral part of your brand's evolving story.

## Getting Familiar with Google Ads Interface

The Google Ads interface is a crucial center for creating and managing your advertising campaigns with accuracy and competence, so learning how to use it is an important adventure into a full digital platform.

At first glance, this dashboard looks like a control room since it has so many features to help you direct your advertising efforts. It's a centralized hub for all of your digital marketing operations, where you can plan, launch, and track your campaigns.

Building a campaign is like preparing a site for your digital projects. Campaign objectives, ad group structures, and other nitty-gritty details may all be crafted here. Planning the structure of your advertising story is essential.

This digital city's structure is reflected in the categorization of ad groups. Each ad group functions like a separate neighborhood, housing advertising and keywords that are specifically targeted to a subset of users in order to maximize relevance and resonance.

Navigation in this virtual world is accomplished using keywords and targeting features. Here you may tailor your messages to your audience's specific requirements and interests, leading them in the direction of your products and services.

You may examine how your advertisements will appear in the context of the overall search results by using the "Ad Preview and Diagnosis" area as an inspection window. Having your advertising content double-checked for coherence and appeal is like the final step before opening your doors to the public.

The reports and performance indicators you generate serve as the map you use to navigate this virtual metropolis. Here, you study the detailed data, evaluating the landscapes traveled by your campaigns and plotting the way for future tactics.

Added functionality, such clickable links or customizable callout extensions, allows you to further customize your campaigns. Your advertising message will have more of an effect with these additions since they improve the user experience.

It takes more than familiarity with the interface's tabs and features to become an expert user; rather, it's a skill to use the interface's tools and insights to create effective campaigns. The ability to communicate in the language of metrics is crucial for gaining actionable intelligence and informing strategic planning for the future.

This user interface serves as much than just a dashboard; it's also a hive of activity for various forms of advertising. Successfully navigating its complexities calls for a head for strategy and a hand for detail, paving the way for the development of informed and persuasive campaigns that leave a lasting impression on their target demographic.

# Chapter 2: Keyword Researching and Writing Compelling Copies

Conducting keyword research and organizing ad campaigns in Google Ads is analogous to designing a building's blueprint; it's a process that combines analytical dexterity with creative accuracy to guarantee that your ads will appeal to the people you're trying to reach.

The core of this method is keyword research, a methodical investigation of search words and phrases that resonate with users. The goal is to find keywords that accurately express user intentions, desires, and the substance of your services, much like a professional explorer looking for buried gold.

These keywords act as a beacon, leading customers directly to your digital door.

Building a solid advertising campaign around these terms is a lot like constructing a structure. It's all about structure and importance. Ad groups, tailored to answer certain user questions, live under the theme wing of each advertising campaign.

This methodical arrangement facilitates targeted messaging, which in turn guarantees that each advertisement will have maximum impact on its target demographic.

Campaign ad groups are carefully created areas that house certain commercials, just like a city planner develops districts with unique qualities. Ad groups allow you to target certain subsets of your audience with tailored message that more closely meets their interests and demands.

These advertising strategies are like beautiful works of architecture; they are meticulously planned to not only attract attention but also lead people on a logical and pertinent path. Getting your message out effectively depends on targeting the right people at the appropriate time.

The filters that further narrow your target audience are the keyword match kinds. They determine how broadly or narrowly your adverts are displayed in response to a user's search that contains your chosen keywords.

But this approach is not simply about compiling a list of keywords or building campaigns—it's about studying user behavior. It's about learning as much as possible about your target demographic so that you may tailor your advertising to their specific interests and demands.

Science and art, accuracy and creativity, go hand in hand when formulating the optimal combination of keywords and organizing advertising campaigns. It's about understanding the user's motivations and then crafting a story that answers their questions and satisfies their needs.

To succeed in the intricate and fascinating world of keyword research and campaign structure, it's not enough to simply have a large number of keywords or well-organized ad groups. Instead, you need to create a harmonious blend of messaging and relevance that complements the user's digital journey.

## Understanding Keyword Research

Beginning with Google Ads' basic keyword research is like setting out on an investigation, a painstaking hunt to decipher the lingo of consumers' search intent so that you may tailor your ads to their wants.

The foundation of this investigation is keyword study, which resembles a treasure hunt in which the goal is to discover the words and phrases that people use to find their way across the Internet. It's more than just a word game; it requires you to put yourself in the shoes of your readers and listen carefully to their concerns and questions.

The first step is figuring out who you're writing for and what they care about. You may learn more about them and their needs by analyzing the search terms they use and the patterns they exhibit.

Finding these terms is like finding a beacon in the huge sea of internet searches, leading customers directly to your virtual front door. They are the backbone of any advertising campaign since they connect your company's name with the words people use while searching for answers.

Broad match, phrase match, and exact match all work as filters to help you narrow down your approach and show your advertising to the most relevant people possible. They mold the contours of your reach, enabling you to throw a wide net or home in on specific user questions.

The skill of keyword research, however, goes well beyond data collecting; it requires a keen eye and the ability to pivot quickly. As user behavior shifts and the seasons transition, so too do fashions. Monitoring these changes will keep your keyword database up-to-date and relevant in the ever-changing digital landscape.

Keyword research isn't only about generating a list of phrases; it's a deep knowledge of human intent, an exercise in empathy and anticipation. Understanding the unstated desires of the audience and crafting a story that speaks to their journey is essential.

In this competitive environment, knowing your target and speaking their language fluently is more important than ever when it comes to keyword research. It's about making it easy for customers to get to the heart of what you're selling by connecting their needs with your brand's answers.

## How to Structure Your Ad Campaigns

Ad campaigns in Google Ads require the same careful planning and organization as any well-crafted story: they must capture the spirit of your business while simultaneously enticing and directing your audience down a path of relevance and resonance.

Campaign structure is the skeleton upon which your advertising narrative emerges. It's much more than just placing advertising where people can see them. Each campaign acts as an overarching theme, incorporating related advertisements and keywords. It's much like a book, with each chapter focusing on a different target demographic or feature of your business.

Ad sections function here like chapters in a book. Advertisements and associated keywords that appeal to a narrow subset of your audience or deal with a specific facet of your organization can be housed in these carefully crafted locations. Each ad group acts as a miniature version of your overall campaign, catered to the unique needs and preferences of a specific fraction of your target audience.

Each section contains examples of advertising copy and creatives. It's not simply the text and images; it's the story that draws people in and communicates your brand's values. Each chapter, or ad group, will engage and resonate with its target audience more effectively if the material is well crafted.

Advertising campaigns are more than just a collection of commercials; they require careful planning to create a seamless experience for the target audience. It's about communicating with the appropriate audience at the right moment.

Further, ad campaigns and ad groups must be organized in a hierarchical structure for efficient administration and optimization. A well-structured campaign is like a well-organized book; it helps you maintain command and improves your capacity to target certain demographics with your message.

The process of testing and improving these structures is analogous to editing and revising a manuscript, with the end goal of increasing the efficacy of ad groups and individual ads. Adapting a story to the changing tastes and expectations of your target audience is an ongoing process.

It's not enough to just arrange items inside Google Ads to create an effective ad campaign; you also need to weave a tale that speaks to your target demographic, leading them on an interesting journey that makes them care about your brand and motivates them to take action.

## Writing Compelling Ad Copies

Copywriting in Google Ads is a lot like writing a story: it requires a deft combination of art and strategy to capture the attention of your target audience and motivate them to take action.

Ad text serves as the conduit via which you convey the essence of your business and lure your target demographic. Ad copywriting requires careful consideration of word choice and arrangement in order to not only attract attention but also leave a lasting impression on the reader.

Each piece of advertising content is a portal into your brand's universe, a chance to connect with consumers and sway their opinions. It's not enough to only provide facts; you also need to arouse interest and motivate people to take action. To achieve this goal, a good balance must be struck between originality and clarity so that the message is both engaging and timely.

Like the first lines of a novel, catchy headlines are essential for getting people interested in what you have to say. They ought to get to the point quickly but also entice the reader to learn more about what you have to offer.

The main body of the ad content conveys the most important information and selling point. Communicating your brand's USPs and solutions in a way that captivates your target market by speaking directly to their pain spots and goals is essential.

A call-to-action (CTA) works as the climax—the key point when you ask the viewer to take action. The success of every call to action (CTA), whether it is a click, a signup, or a purchase, hinges on how well it is written.

To further enhance the advertising experience, ad extensions may be thought of as supplemental chapters within the main plot. They improve the story, providing customers with more opportunities to interact with your company.

Copywriting isn't simply about stringing words together; it's about tapping into your target market's hopes and fears to create an effective pitch. It's not just about making a sale; it's about making an impact and getting people to take action.

In the competitive world of advertising copy, the ability to convey a tale that sticks with the reader is crucial. Advertising copywriting is more than simply talking up a product; it's also about starting a conversation and drawing readers into your brand's backstory.

## Understanding the Impact of Ads Extension

Adding ad extensions to your Google Ads campaigns is like adding a new chapter to your ad's story; it's a great way to expand on your core message and pique the interest of your target audience.

Ad extensions add new dimensions to your advertising narrative. They help your ad reach more people, get more people to take action, and give them additional ways to interact with your company.

Sitelink extensions, for example, function as in-text links that direct readers to the sections of your website most likely to pique their interest. These add-ons serve as alternative routes, leading searchers straight to the content that is most relevant to their questions.

Extensions to callouts serve as footnotes, enhancing the story by bringing attention to additional advantages or distinguishing features. They highlight the finer points that help to differentiate your company and its service from the competitors.

Structured snippet extensions serve as subplots, enhancing the narrative by highlighting particular facets of your offerings. Users benefit from their increased knowledge, and the ad is better for it.

Similar to a story's setting, the location extension provides geographical background for the reader. They help customers discover your stores in the real world by giving them crucial information about your locations.

Call and message extensions serve as the narrative's interactive dialogue by providing customers with additional ways to get in touch with your company. They stimulate instant action, urging people to phone, chat, or interact immediately with your company.

Ad extensions provide a wide range of effects. They improve the user experience while simultaneously increasing ad space and exposure. By giving extra information and more options to engage, ad extensions boost the likelihood of people interacting with your ad, hence raising click-through rates and conversion rates.

In addition, ads that make use of ad extensions tend to perform better in terms of rank and placement. Successful use of several ad extensions can boost an ad's position in search engine results, so increasing its exposure and, hopefully, its click-through rate.

Ad extensions aren't simply extras; they help you give your viewers a more comprehensive and interesting ad experience. It's like adding additional detail to a tale; it makes the user's experience and interactions with your business better.

## Chapter 3: How to Increase Reach in Google Ads

"Reach" in Google Ads is a crucial number that evaluates the possibility and scope of engaging with your audience throughout Google's huge network, and understanding it is equivalent to understanding the breadth and depth of your advertising influence.

The term "reach" refers to the total number of people that might potentially see your advertisement during a certain time frame. It's not just about how many people see your ad or how many times they click it.

In this advertising tale, "Reach" is the imprint left by your brand's presence in search, display, video, and partner sites. It specifies how many people might see your ad and gives you a rough idea of how many people might interact with your campaign.

Reach may be defined as the extent to which your audience is exposed to your content. Reaching a wide variety of people who are likely to be interested in your product is more important than simply increasing the number of people who see your ad. It gives you an idea of how big and varied your prospective audience is in the places you're considering.

Reach is affected by a wide range of variables, including demographics, geography, interest, and medium. The possible Reach of your advertisement is directly affected by the choices you choose here. Ad targeting is the process of adjusting your settings so that your ad appears before the appropriate people at the correct time.

The significance of Reach goes beyond simple numerical analysis to consider the full breadth of your advertising's potential influence. It aids in decision-making, letting you better plan and manage resources so that your ad reaches the most applicable consumers.

You can modify your advertising tactics based on what you learn about Reach. It's a measure that may help you figure out whether your targeting options are too wide or too specific, and whether or not they mesh well with your campaign goals and target groups.

In addition, when combined with data like frequency and impressions, Reach may reveal how often certain individuals are exposed to your ad. You may use this information to find the sweet spot between audience exposure and ad fatigue as you fine-tune your campaign.

Understanding Reach in today's advertising market is about more than just statistics; it's about gauging the potential impact of your brand in the digital sphere. It's a map that helps you find your way around the large Google Ads system, where you can fine-tune your strategies to reach the right people and raise your brand's profile in the process.

## Benefits of Audience Reach

Google Ads' Audience Reach is a fundamental indicator that emphasizes your message's ability to connect and interact with the appropriate individuals in the digital arena, making it the cornerstone of effective advertising.

Reaching an audience is more than just a metric; it represents the effectiveness of your marketing. It's a measure of how many distinct members of your intended audience will see your ad. The key is to zero in on the people who are most likely to be interested in what you have to offer, and build meaningful relationships with them.

Advertising's epic story may be navigated with the help of Audience Reach. You may use it to gauge how well your ad will perform in front of a given demographic. Reaching a large number of people is important, but so is getting your message in front of the people who are most likely to convert.

The power of Audience Reach resides in how precisely you can narrow your focus. It's all about zeroing in on a certain audience based on their characteristics, habits, interests, and goals. With such pinpoint accuracy, your ad will only be seen to those who are truly interested in what you have to offer.

Creating unique advertising encounters is an integral part of expanding a campaign's reach. It's all about making sure your message fits the wants, expectations, and actions of your intended audience. Your ad is more likely to generate interest and conversions thanks to the customization.

Audience Reach analysis also lets you evaluate advertising success and make course corrections. It tells you how well your targeting options are working, and from there you can decide whether to broaden or limit your audience groups for the best possible interaction.

Audience Reach has far-reaching consequences. It helps your brand get seen and gets most out of your advertising dollar. Focusing on the right people will cut down on impressions wasted on uninterested users and increase conversions from those who are actually interested in what you have to offer.

Reaching a large number of people isn't as important as getting your message in front of the appropriate people, according to this account of advertising strategy. Marketing efforts may benefit greatly from this strategic strategy since it allows them to reach the people who are most likely to be interested in them.

## How Targeting Impact Maximizing Reach

Your advertising efforts would be lost without targeting as your guide. It's all about zeroing in on the subset of consumers who will get the most out of your brand's products. Advertisers may deliberately target the people most likely to engage with and convert by using targeting characteristics like demographics, interests, behaviors, and geography.

When you know how to target your campaign to the most appropriate audience subgroups, you can increase your reach.

Those who are actively looking for a service or product like the one you provide are the ones you want to target. Ads may only be seen to those who are truly interested in what you have to offer if you use targeting to narrow down your audience.

In addition to ensuring that the correct individuals are reached, targeting also helps ensure that the wrong people are avoided. By not showing your advertising to people who aren't in the target demographic or who don't have your interests, you may save money and increase the effectiveness of your campaign.

Customization and customization of ad material are also made possible by dynamic and accurate targeting. Targeting guarantees that the ad strongly resonates with the targeted audience by personalizing the content to the needs, desires, and habits of certain audience groups, hence generating higher engagement and increased conversion potential.

Reach may be significantly increased with precise aiming. It simplifies ad distribution, so your message only goes to the people who are most likely to convert, increasing the effectiveness of your ad and your ROI.

The story of advertising strategy relies heavily on the function of targeting. It's a resource that helps marketers zero in on the areas where they'll see the most return on investment, like reaching out to the people most likely to be receptive to their advertisements.

# Chapter 4: Targeting Techniques for Staying Relevant

Appropriate targeting tactics in Google Ads lead marketers to their target demographic with pinpoint accuracy. Campaigns are better able to reach their target demographics when they are aligned with the most relevant audience groups using these methods.

Understanding and dividing up your target demographic are the keys to a successful targeting strategy. Demographics include things like age, gender, income, and level of education, whereas psychographics include things like personality and online activity.

This in-depth knowledge equips marketers with the tools they need to create segment-specific communications.

Using a person's location data, advertising may target just those people in that area. Geographic targeting allows you to send your message directly to the individuals who are most likely to be interested in it, whether that's on a worldwide scale or inside a certain nation, city, or radius.

Understanding user behavior is crucial to behavioral targeting tactics. This may include users' historical behaviors, such as interactions, purchases, or content engagements. By taking use of these patterns, campaigns may be developed that are tailored to the interests and preferences of individual consumers.

Interest-based targeting caters to individuals based on their individual likes and dislikes. Advertisers may target the perfect audience by learning more about their preferences in terms of content, websites visited, and other demographic information.

Ads are served to viewers when they are viewing information on a given topic via contextual targeting. This technique capitalizes on the content people are actively engaged with, ensuring that the ad is relevant and connected with the context of the material being consumed.

Users who have already engaged with a website or app are the focus of remarketing and retargeting campaigns. These methods of advertising communicate directly to those who have showed an interest in the brand by targeting just those people who have shown an interest in the products or services in question.

Targeting methods for relevance aren't just about reaching as many people as possible; they're also about making meaningful connections with the best possible subsets of your target audience.

These methods provide marketers the ability to target specific audiences with messaging that will have a greater chance of striking a chord, leading to deeper engagement and more successful sales.

They're essential for making sure ads are tailored to each individual viewer and address their interests and concerns.

## Understanding Audience Targeting

Reaching the right people at the right moment might be a mystery, but demystifying audience targeting in Google Ads is all about uncovering those mysteries. By taking into account a wide range of factors, audience targeting may ensure that commercials reach the right people and have a profound effect on them.

The foundation of effective audience targeting is a thorough familiarity with your target demographics. Advertisers may target specific audiences based on characteristics like age, gender, income, and level of education.

One further component is learning about the demographic and psychographic details of your target market.

To do so, you must investigate their likes, dislikes, habits, and inclinations. Advertisers may increase the usefulness of their material by targeting certain demographic groups by learning what appeals to each group.

Geographic targeting is also significant. Its goal is to connect with people in specific geographic areas, whether that's on a global scale, in a single city or region, or in a more localized setting. With this method, your message will be tailored to each user's specific location.

Understanding a user's activities while interacting with a website is the key to successful behavioral targeting. This information is used to tailor campaigns to each individual user based on their behavior and interests.

Contextual targeting is the practice of delivering advertisements in settings pertinent to the material with which consumers are interacting at any one time. Ads are more likely to be relevant and interesting if they are contextualized inside the content being viewed.

Retargeting, also known as remarketing, is reaching out to people who have already interacted with a website or mobile app. By interacting with these people again, brands may increase their audience's affinity for and knowledge of their products.

Defining broad audiences is only the first step in audience targeting; the second step is to deconstruct these audiences into small groups with shared qualities or habits. It's an art that relies on knowing your audience inside and out so you can communicate with them in ways that are relevant, engaging, and consistent with who they are as individuals.

## Using Keywords and Ad Groups for Reach

Keyword and ad group strategic interaction is an artistic cornerstone in the ever-changing world of digital marketing, signaling the intensity of a brand's reach. Using this synergy, advertisers can steer their way through the digital world and craft an exciting adventure that will keep their target consumers captivated and moving forward.

Keywords are the fundamental codes that unlock the maze of online purpose and are thus central to this orchestration. These keywords, which have been carefully crafted, act as a compass, leading campaigns directly to the sought-after niches of relevance. They disclose the latent needs, goals, and questions of the digital populous, creating a route through which marketers resonate with their audience.

Ad groups are included with these keywords; they are thorough compilations that transform the energy of the keywords into compelling stories. In order to attract customers, these advertising agencies transform simple text into stirring narratives. By weaving together the searcher's motivations and the brand's persuasive answer, they create a captivating narrative.

Using keywords and ad groups to expand your audience is an exercise in accuracy and dexterity. It's a place where carefully chosen keywords and cleverly arranged ad groups work in harmony to lead consumers along a path that answers their questions and fulfills their needs.

By using this formula, companies may open up new opportunities much beyond the scope of simple exposure. They create experiences that go beyond the bounds of conventional advertising, ushering in a time of more individualization and deeper connections between brands and their consumers.

The challenge is in mastering the art of comprehension, which entails discerning the subtleties of user intent, carving out the contours of relevance, and creating a fully immersive, anticipatory, and fulfilling experience. Extending the digital touchpoints to their full potential requires mastery of a harmonic balance of the proper keywords inside well-structured ad groups, resulting in an alluring journey that resonates with each user's unique inquiry and develops a lasting relationship.

## Unleashing the Power of Location Targeting

Location targeting is a game-changer in the modern business world since it enables companies to target certain populations and regions with highly targeted marketing campaigns. A thorough comprehension of customer behavior, preferences, and the contextual dynamics surrounding them is at the heart of this precision marketing method, which goes well beyond a simple map-based plan.

Because of its capability to decode complex behavioral patterns, location targeting can provide a more in-depth insight of how customers interact with their environments. Using this information, companies may improve their goods, services, and advertising to better meet the needs of their target demographic.

Location targeting has revolutionized several industries, including the distribution of targeted advertisements, the management of supply chains, and the improvement of service provision. To achieve unprecedented levels of reach, consumer engagement, and operational efficiency, businesses are increasingly turning to this technology.

The skill of harnessing the potential of location targeting isn't only about identifying consumers; it's about knowing them—where they are, what they prefer, and how they engage. This knowledge motivates companies to not only respond to but also anticipate the requirements of their target market, giving them a leg up in the marketplace by providing relevant, personalized experiences.

Whil hen it comes to Google Ads, the most cost-effective methods are those that make the most of available resources without sacrificing results. The primary goal of these strategies is to maximize outcomes while minimizing costs, making the most of every available dollar.

Setting defined marketing objectives and goals is key to a cost-effective approach. The success of every marketing effort depends on setting precise, quantifiable targets, such as raising brand recognition, increasing website traffic, or boosting conversions.

Allocating funds wisely is crucial. It's crucial to know how to allocate funds for optimum effect. Spending may be optimized and targeted activities that fit with your aims via the use of cost-effective bidding tactics like automated bidding or bid modifications.

In order to maximize efficiency, keyword targeting must be used properly. By using the right keywords and avoiding the wrong ones, advertisers may target just the people who are truly interested in their products.

A cost-effective strategy is to regularly review and optimize campaigns. Measuring and analyzing key performance indicators enables swift, well-informed action. Improve the efficacy and cost-effectiveness of your efforts by weeding out what isn't working and expanding on what is.

Using geo-targeting and ad scheduling, you can get your message in front of your ideal customers when and where they are most receptive to it. This targeted method makes the most of your advertising dollars by showing your adverts only when your intended audience is online and ready to interact with them.

Ad extensions are another low-cost tactic. As a consequence, they improve ad content and interaction at no extra expense, leading to a greater return on investment.

Optimizing content strategically is crucial for saving money. Ad quality may be increased, prices decreased, and ad placement enhanced via the use of creative writing, ad testing, and landing page optimization.

A/B testing and continual experimentation help advertisers to determine the most effective techniques. Ad formats, targeting choices, and messaging may all be tested to see what works best for a certain campaign's goals and budget.

Smart planning, constant optimization, and strategic execution are the three pillars of a cost-effective Google Ads strategy. It's not enough to merely cut expenses; you also need to make sure that every dollar you put into advertising yields a positive return and aids in the overall success of your campaign.

## Budgeting for Gaining Optimal Reach

In the huge realm of digital marketing, money allocation plays a significant part in defining the success and effect of a brand's online presence. To efficiently reach the correct audience, every decision on where to distribute finances is like sailing a ship in an ocean.

Budget allocation may be thought of as a spell. You have a set of components, and the way you combine them determines the outcome. The key is to strategically spread your resources over many internet communities, each of which has its own audience and selling point.

The first stage is gaining familiarity with these systems. Some, like social media, are like thriving downtowns where people meet, talk, and trade tales. Some, like search engines and e-commerce sites, serve as virtual equivalents to brick-and-mortar bookstores and libraries. Each medium has its own personality, so it's important to focus your marketing dollars where they'll have the most impact.

But it's not only about finding the perfect spot; it's also about knowing your audience. Picture this as learning what kind of music partygoers prefer. It's important to put money where your target demographic already spends time online. It's vital to know what they like, how they act, and where they hang out online.

Choosing how much to spend is like picking what to choose from a buffet after you know where to place your money. You have to strike a good middle ground. You shouldn't put all of your money into one area while ignoring the others. This calls for some experimentation, testing, and close monitoring of results.

Let me explain why this is about more than simply cash. money's about spending money intelligently. Money must be put to good use. It's not enough to simply display advertisements; you also need to make moments that resonate with your target demographic. It's less of an announcement and more of an exchange of ideas.

Allocating a digital marketing budget for maximum impact requires forethought, flexibility, and awareness of your target demographic. Marketing is the practice of getting the most out of your available means, spreading your brand's message to the people who need to hear it and in the ways they like to receive it.

## Cost-Efficient, Smart Bidding Techniques

Businesses who are serious about improving their online visibility recognize the critical importance of optimizing their digital advertising budgets to the fullest extent possible. A shining light in this landscape, smart bidding tactics use a data-driven approach to managing and optimizing advertising campaigns.

To get the most out of each ad placement while staying under budget, smart bidding techniques use machine learning and data analysis to make automated, real-time modifications to the bids. This clever method takes into account things like the user's gadget, physical location, time of day, and past actions in order to place accurate bids.

Smart bidding's true genius is in its capacity to learn and change over time. These methods can quickly modify bids by assessing past data and monitoring current performance, with the goal of optimizing conversions or other campaign objectives within a certain budget.

The final result is advertising budgets that are highly optimized, making every dollar go farther by targeting the right people at the right time with the appropriate message. This effectiveness not only reduces the amount of money wasted on advertising, but also makes the advertising budget go farther and has a greater return on investment.

Finally, firms are given the keys to unlocking advertising cost-efficiency through the incorporation of smart bidding tactics. It's not only about saving money; it's about investing it better, enabling campaigns to adapt dynamically, giving optimal outcomes while maintaining a tight control on expenses. By redefining digital advertising's efficiency and efficacy with the use of technology, those that take advantage of it may gain a competitive edge.

Assessing the efficacy of your Google Ads campaigns requires collecting and analyzing relevant data. To ensure your campaigns are successful, it is important to measure their impact and efficacy using a number of key performance indicators (KPIs).

The first step in evaluating achievement is setting clear and explicit objectives. Having clear goals establishes a standard of success, whether the aim is to increase brand recognition, website traffic, or the number of conversions.

Success may be measured with the use of key performance indicators (KPIs). Essential indicators for evaluating campaign success include click-through rates (CTRs), conversion rates, cost per acquisition (CPA), return on ad spend (ROAS), and quality score. These indicators give insights into user engagement, conversion efficacy, cost-efficiency, and overall ad quality.

Examining these indicators can shed light on the areas of success and failure. Monitoring output over time allows for the discovery of patterns, trends, and development opportunities. Data analysis allows for more educated choices to be made about the development and improvement of plans and campaigns.

The client lifecycle cannot be comprehended without utilizing attribution modeling. First-click, last-click, linear, and temporal decay are just some of the attribution models available for determining which marketing channels are most responsible for a given transaction. The effectiveness of plans and resource allocation may be improved by identifying the most important touchpoints.

Information from Google Ads may be supplemented with additional details by using Google Analytics. You can see the full impact of your advertising on user actions and conversions by connecting these platforms and getting a fuller picture of user behavior and website performance.

Adopting performance benchmarks and comparisons to industry norms assists in analyzing the efficacy of your initiatives. You may acquire a better understanding of your successes and areas for growth by comparing them to those of your peers or the industry as a whole.

Success evaluation is a continual procedure. The key to long-term success is to constantly test and iterate tactics, adjust to market shifts, and refine your strategy based on observations. Maximizing the impact and efficiency of your advertising requires you to have a nimble, responsive, and proactive mindset.

In conclusion, evaluating the efficacy of your Google Ads campaigns requires a thorough examination of a number of measures, the alignment of your performance with clearly articulated goals, and the ongoing adjustment of your strategy.

## Indicators for Evaluating Reach

In the convoluted terrain of digital marketing, understanding the main indicators for analyzing reach is like deciphering a treasure map that uncovers the success and effect of a brand's online initiatives. These indicators are like road signs, leading marketers to an understanding of their digital footprint's length, breadth, and depth.

Picture these indicators as checkpoints along a path. These metrics provide valuable insight into the reach, interest, and impact of your message. They serve as milestones against which you can gauge the success of your strategies and make course corrections as necessary.

'Impressions' is the first essential measure; it's the equivalent of the number of times someone gazed at a billboard. The number of times your article was seen indicates how many impressions it received. While this isn't conclusive evidence, it does provide some insight into how many people saw your material.

In the future, 'Reach' will be synonymous with counting the number of people that saw your material. It's like trying to guess how many people glanced at the billboard as they passed it.

Estimating your audience size and the percentage of people you were able to reach is what reach does for you.

'Engagement' is another indicator that may tell you whether or not your audience did anything more than casually browse. It's the equivalent of tallying the number of individuals who looked at a billboard and, maybe, snapped a photo of it. Likes, shares, comments, and other indicators that your audience is engaged with your material online are all examples of engagement.

The rate of conversion is another important indicator. Think of it as knowing how many people saw the billboard, stopped to read it, and then either made a purchase or entered the store. The conversion rate reflects the proportion of website visitors who took the intended course of action, such as making a purchase or subscribing to a service.

In addition, the 'Click-Through Rate (CTR)' is the proportion of recipients who not only saw but also interacted with your message. It's the same as the number of individuals who encountered the billboard and took action in response to it by photographing it.

The fourth, crucial indicator is 'ROI' - Return on Investment. It's the equivalent of calculating how much money was made thanks to that billboard. A digital marketing campaign's ROI demonstrates whether or not the time and energy spent on it is paying off.

These critical indicators for gauging reach in digital marketing are the beacon that helps marketers find their way in the enormous sea of information. Marketers may learn a lot about their content's reception, level of engagement, and success in inspiring the targeted actions by analyzing these indicators. They're not simply statistics; they're indications pointing the way to a digital strategy that works better and more efficiently.

## KPI and ROI Evaluation

Businesses may find their way through the maze of their goals and actions by analyzing performance through KPIs and Return on Investment (ROI). These measurements are the foundation of good judgment since they shed light on how successful and efficient an endeavor has been.

Customized KPIs establish measurable standards against which progress may be tracked. Sales, customer acquisition, lead creation, and other measurable objectives may be tracked with ease. Key performance indicators (KPIs) serve as guides, showing whether or not a business is on track to achieve its goals.

Meanwhile, return on investment assesses how useful and profitable a financial outlay was. It measures the profitability of projects by comparing their returns to their expenditures. Return on investment (ROI) is an essential metric for evaluating the efficacy and worth of a given activity by comparing the amount gained to the amount spent on that action.

Key performance indicators and return on investment (ROI) work together to paint a whole picture of a company's success or failure. Key performance indicators (KPIs) point in the right direction, while return on investment (ROI) proves that the work was worth the money.

Together, they help decision-makers determine which tactics provide the greatest return on investment so that they may allocate resources and plan their future actions accordingly.

Further, firms may capitalize on productive initiatives while abandoning ineffective ones thanks to continuing study and comprehension of these data. Measuring, analyzing, and adjusting in a cycle helps a company develop and innovate over time.

To measure performance and guide future efforts toward higher efficiency, effectiveness, and overall success in today's highly competitive and continuously changing corporate scene, the symbiotic link between KPIs and ROI is a vital tool.

## Chapter 7: Be Flexible and Stay in Control

With Google Ads, marketers can fine-tune their campaigns, respond quickly to shifts in the market, and perfect their optimization techniques thanks to the platform's adaptability and control. This feature gives advertisers a great deal of control over their ads, letting them make changes and tweaks for optimal results.

The ability to make changes to campaigns in real time is a major perk. Rapidly adapting to new market conditions and shifting consumer preferences by adjusting ad text, bidding methods, and targeting settings in real time.

Advertisers need a lot of leeway in their budgets. Advertisers may better optimize their spending by reallocating funds from weak regions to those showing promise, all thanks to real-time budget allocation adjustments.

Targeting control is a key tool inside Google Ads. Marketers may target particular subsets of consumers based on characteristics like age, gender, location, and hobbies. The most relevant and active users will see your ads thanks to this pinpoint targeting.

The ability to schedule advertisements is another convenient option. Ads may be scheduled to run at specified times of day or on specific days of the week, increasing the likelihood that the target audience will see the ad at just the right time.

Ads may be made more relevant to certain regions of the world thanks to geo-targeting technology. By tailoring their messages to certain regions, advertisers may boost the effectiveness of their efforts.

With the use of A/B testing, businesses can try out several versions of their ads and see which ones perform better in terms of things like headlines, pictures, and calls to action. Campaign refinement and improvement benefit from this test-driven approach.

Advertisers have more say over their ads thanks to customizable ad extensions. Utilizing extensions like as sitelinks, callouts, or structured snippets allows the option to add more information, improving the ad experience and boosting interaction.

Advertisers may be quick to react thanks to Google Ads' adaptability and control features. It allows them the flexibility to adjust their advertising tactics, make educated judgments, and fine-tune their campaigns based on real-time data and performance indicators, all of which guarantees that their ads will be targeted, efficient, and in line with their objectives.

## Customize Your For Enhanced Reach

Imagine ad customization as a personal letter. You wouldn't use generic language in a letter to a buddy. Based on your audience and your goals, you craft a unique message. In a similar vein, ad customization entails tailoring your message to certain demographics or interests.

Identifying your target demographic is the first step. This is like to meeting someone and immediately recognizing them. Do they look young? Do they care more about the latest trends or cutting-edge gadgets? Having this information allows you to better target your message.

The actual words used in your advertisement. Modifying the text to fit the target audience increases the likelihood that the message will resonate with them. It's as if you were having a discussion with your friend, using language and expressions shared by the two of you.

The use of images and other visual aids is also crucial. The pattern on your clothing, if you will. Everyone has their own unique sense of style. The preference for muted tones may be shared by those who enjoy brighter hues. Customizing graphics involves responding to those tastes, making sure your ad appears nice and resonates with your target.

Another important part is the "Call to Action" (CTA). It's like having a discussion with a buddy and then asking them to do something afterward. Whether you want them to join up, buy something, or just learn more, a well-crafted call to action can help you get there. The goal is to guide them to the next stage of their adventure.

It's also important to tailor where your ads appear. It's like picking the ideal spot to have a chat with a buddy, whether it's a lively cafe, a serene park, or a quiet library. In the digital realm, it's about determining where your ad will be viewed - on social media, search engines, or specific websites where your target spends their time.

Ad personalization for increased reach is, in essence, tailoring your message to certain subsets of your target audience. It's about making sure your message is interesting and engaging to the people you want to hear it and get them to take action. Ad personalization, like a well-fitting suit, increases the likelihood that your target audience will notice and respond positively to your message.

## Methods for Optimizing Your Campaign

Fine-tuning marketing tactics for optimal efficiency and success requires the use of campaign optimization for control. They cover a variety of approaches and procedures focused towards retaining a tight grasp on the performance and direction of a campaign.

The most common of these methods is known as "A/B testing," and it's used to conduct scientifically controlled trials that compare two versions of an element inside a campaign. Ad creatives, content variants, audience segmentation, and landing page designs may all be tested with A/B testing to see which ones perform better with the intended audience.

In addition, using analytics and data-tracking tools is crucial for managing your campaign effectively. Marketers can quickly discover failing areas and make instant modifications by monitoring critical data in real time, such as click-through rates, conversions, engagement levels, and bounce rates. By keeping a close eye, we can make sure the campaign is still on track and use that information to make informed judgments about how to improve its performance.

Campaign control also includes allocating resources and setting a schedule. Spending may be optimized by regularly analyzing and redistributing the money in response to the performance of various parts within the campaign. Allocating funds to the most productive channels and activities is only possible with real-time control and balancing of the budget.

In addition, a large part of campaign management is ensuring that all brand messages are consistent and that all marketing channels are working together cohesively. This ensures that the campaign's core values are upheld and that consumers have a consistent and engaging interaction with the brand across all mediums.

By applying these optimization approaches for control, firms may adjust and optimize their efforts on-the-go, producing incremental changes that cumulatively boost the campaign's overall success. The campaign will continue to be effective, efficient, and adaptable to the ever-changing demands of the audience thanks to this ongoing process of optimization.

# Chapter 8: Industry Best Practices

E-commerce: E-commerce firms that employ dynamic remarketing have been the focus of several successful case studies. Companies saw substantial gains in conversion rates when they showed targeted advertising featuring previously seen items to site visitors who did not make a purchase. Ads that were personalized based on user activity saw a rise in clickthrough rates and sales.

Case studies showed the success that local firms may have by utilizing hyper-local targeting. Businesses were able to reach their target audiences in the best possible context by integrating location-based targeting with ad timing. The outcome was a rise in foot traffic and sales.

Lead Generation with Lead advertisements: Various businesses, such as B2B services or education, achieved success by implementing lead advertisements.

Ads that integrated lead forms improved user experience, leading to more qualified leads and more sales. These efforts were fruitful in that they attracted attention and collected data from possible buyers.

App install campaigns: businesses who wanted to increase app downloads used Google Ads to do it. Companies saw substantial boosts in app downloads and installs by employing app-specific ad formats and targeting users based on their interests and habits.

Donations were boosted thanks to Google Ads used by charitable groups. Non-profits were able to raise more money and spread their messages to more people because to the advertising funding they received.

These real-world examples and illustrative case studies showcase effective techniques for using Google Ads. There are examples of dynamic remarketing, hyper-local targeting, lead advertisements, app install campaigns, and non-profit advertising grants, all of which were employed by different companies and organizations to attain their goals and generate the most possible engagement and sales. Accurate targeting, powerful message, and smart use of Google Ads capabilities and tools contributed to the success of these efforts.

## Brands Success Stories

The "Share a Coke" advertising campaign by Coca-Cola was a smashing success. The campaign's goal was to form more meaningful relationships with customers by allowing them to put their names on the things they purchased. More sales and more exposure for the brand among the younger generation resulted from this strategy's enhanced brand engagement and wider reach.

Using comedy and a recognizable figure, Old Spice was able to improve their brand's appeal among younger audiences with their renowned "The Man Your Man Could Smell Like" campaign. As a result, it was picked up by a lot of other media, which boosted interest and ultimately sales.

Dove's "Real Beauty Sketches" campaign spoke out about social concerns and sought to alter conventional notions of physical attractiveness. The content's ability to evoke strong feelings in its viewers led to widespread distribution and attention from people all over the world.

During the Olympic period, P&G promoted their "Thank You, Mom" ad. This touching series of commercials highlighted the importance of moms in helping their kids achieve their goals. Reaching people on an emotional level, the topic had a significant impact.

Apple's "Get a Mac" Campaign: Apple's series of advertising contrasting a PC with a Mac were incredibly effective in showing the benefits of Mac computers. The campaign's innovative message and comparative approach attracted a lot of people and led to a huge boost in brand awareness.

These campaigns are examples of those that were able to reach a wide audience, pique consumer interest, and substantially raise brand recognition. These advertisements were successful because they had novel ideas, strong emotions, or hilarious aspects that connected with consumers on a deep level.

## Implementing Strategies for Various Industries

Strategy implementation across many sectors calls for a sophisticated approach that takes into account each industry's distinct features, difficulties, and possibilities. While many ideas could have universal relevance, their execution generally needs a personalized and industry-specific approach.

Innovation and fast progress are essential to the success of industries like technology. Strategy execution in this environment calls for nimbleness, a commitment to R&D, and the capacity to respond rapidly to shifting market conditions. Product development and customer experience are typically driven by data-based insights gained from a company's commitment to cultivating an innovative culture and keeping pace with ever evolving technology landscapes.

Compliance with rules and regulations and concern for patients are of paramount importance in healthcare. Strategies should prioritize patient-centered care, digital transformation, and operational efficiency while yet conforming to severe rules. In this field, it is essential to use individualized treatment techniques, electronic health records, and telemedicine.

The retail industry must adopt a customer-first mindset, one that places a premium on tailoring interactions with customers and utilizing data-driven insights to better serve their needs. Integrating online and physical experiences, harnessing technology for frictionless transactions, and utilizing data for targeted marketing and sales are all crucial to the success of any strategy here.

Efficiency in operations, optimization of the supply chain, and environmental responsibility are commonplace in the manufacturing industry. Strategies center on enhancing processes, using lean manufacturing concepts, and adopting Industry 4.0 technologies to boost productivity through things like automation, predictive maintenance, and optimal use of resources.

Trust, security, and a streamlined digital experience are common strategic foci in the banking sector. Adopting new financial technology, strengthening security protocols, and providing individualized financial services informed by big data are all crucial.

A thorough familiarity with the unique difficulties and potentials of one's business is essential for effective strategy implementation. Success and continued competitive advantage depend on developing and implementing strategies that are tailored to the unique challenges faced by each sector. Success in a wide variety of fields requires a high degree of versatility, adaptability, and a readiness to adjust tactics in light of industry specifics.

# Chapter 9: Are You Ready to Take on Google Ads?

Learning Google Ads is a thrilling adventure into the world of online promotion. You should go into it with an open mind and a thirst for information. Learn the fundamentals first, such how the platform works, how to navigate around it, and what terms are often used. Don't be scared to try new things and make errors; that's how you learn.

Stay current with the ever-evolving field of digital marketing. If you want to learn more, look into books, videos, and courses from credible sources. Set up your own campaigns, try out various techniques, and evaluate the outcomes to gain practical experience. Keep in mind that information can help you improve your efforts.

Have persistence and patience. Acing Google Ads takes time and practice. Those that put in the effort and are willing to change will succeed. Don't resist platform updates; they usually bring about exciting new possibilities for development and improvement.

One last thing, keep your mind open to new information. Digital advertising is a fast-paced, ever-evolving industry. Never stop learning, never stop engaging, and never stop being receptive to novel approaches, methods, and fashions. Enjoy the trip; you're in for a thrilling adventure with Google Ads.

Keep in mind that mastering Google Ads is an ongoing process, and that your knowledge and skill will develop in tandem with your experience using the tool. Jump in, learn as you go, be tenacious, and have fun as you become a Google Ads expert.